Why Am I Here?

How To Find Your Purpose And Start Living The Life You Were Meant To Live

MARTIN FORMATO

Disclaimer

The information is of a general nature and does not take into account your personal situation. The information presented is for educational purposes only. The author will not bear any responsibility or liability for any action taken by any person, persons or organization on the purported basis of the information contained in this book and any supporting material. References to other information, websites or events should not be understood as an endorsement of such information, website or events. Every effort has been made to ensure that this book is free from errors or omissions. However, the author shall not accept responsibility for injury, loss or damage occasioned to any person acting or refraining from action as a result of material in this book whether or not such injury, loss or damage is in any way due to any negligent act or omission, breach of duty or default on the part of the author.

DEDICATION

I dedicate this book to my father for giving me a kick when I needed it; and my mother for catching me when I was falling.

CONTENTS

INTRODUCTION

I want to thank you and congratulate you for buying this book, "**Why Am I Here?**"

This book contains proven steps and strategies on how to find your purpose so you can start living the life you were meant to live.

This is not a "get happy quick" trick. This book contains a proven process that will allow you to find your true self so you can create a life you love.

This book all started with the idea that if I can help just one person find out why they are here, then the time I have spent writing this book will have been totally worth it. And it has done just that many times over.

Here is to you and your quest to find out why you are here and create a life you love!

Thanks again for buying this book, I hope you enjoy it!

MY STORY

Hi, I am Martin Formato, a professional certified life and business coach, motivational speaker and author of the self-help book, "**Follow Your Own Path**".

My passion is to inspire you to do what you love that also contributes to humanity. How? By helping you express yourself through your passion.

This process will inevitably result in you creating a life you love.

How would you like to jump out of bed every Monday morning, full of excitement about the day ahead because you a living your life with passion and purpose?

I believe that you are a gift to the world and have a passion, gift, talent, skill or ability of some sort, which, once discovered and developed, will open up a whole new, amazing and wonderful world.

What you can contribute no-one else can contribute, because you are unique.

I want to help you find your passion and develop it so you can give it to the world. Why? Because:

- I get a buzz helping people transform their life,
- The world needs that special something that only you can give,
- You deserve to be happy and when you express yourself through

your passion you will be happy,

- You will love what you do every day and who you are becoming and
- You will create a life you love.

By living your passion, you will also be setting an example for your family and friends to do the same. You will inspire them to also go after their dream.

I imagine a world where most people love Mondays because they love what they do; they express themselves through their passion, they help others and fulfill their dream. It doesn't get any better than that!

My blog at www.martinformato.com is my way of sharing ideas, concepts and principles that I have learnt over the last 50 years, which, if acted upon, will allow you to create a life you love. I am sharing this information as my way of giving back to society.

I am thankful to all those men, women and children that I have met throughout my life; some still living and others deceased; the authors of numerous books I have read; seminars I attended; movies and videos I have watched; audios I have listened to; and especially my parents, sister and brothers, my wife, children and relatives for teaching and helping me to shape the person I have become.

It doesn't matter if you are struggling or doing well, I guarantee that you will learn something from my blog that will make your life better.

My Early Life

I was born to immigrant parents who escaped war torn Italy for a better life in Australia. I am an Aussie Italian.

My father was a laborer and my mother, a cleaner.

I am the youngest of four children.

As a child I was shy, insecure and skinny, and, as a result, I was sometimes teased at school.

Growing up, we did not have much, as money was tight.

At age 12, I got a job selling newspapers. I did that for 4 years and enjoyed it very much. I made some money and learnt a bit about business and people.

When I was not selling newspapers, I hung around my neighborhood with friends till late at night. Often, I would come home to find the door locked. This was done to teach me a lesson. I then had to beg for someone to let me in.

During this period of my life, my father noticed that I was not spending much time doing my school work. He said that I would probably drop out of school and spend the rest of my life looking after sheep. This upset me and made me feel like a loser.

One particular day, I was feeling down, so I went to the city. I walked around aimlessly until I got tired and ended up stopping at a cinema. On the window, I saw a poster of a movie that looked interesting, so I went inside to check it out. The movie was called *Rocky*, a million to one shot about an unknown underdog boxer nicknamed 'The Italian Stallion' who fights the heavyweight champion of the world, Apollo Creed, and unbelievably 'goes the distance' under the direction of wily fight manager Mickey.

This movie blew me away. It made such an impact. I felt a strong connection with the main character, Rocky Balboa. I could see the similarities between his life and my life. I learnt how Rocky went from being a nobody to becoming a somebody. I was inspired. This character gave me hope. I knew that the messages in the movie could help me overcome the challenges in my life. So, Rocky became my first coach.

At that point, I made a decision to do the best I could, given the limited time I had left before my final year 12 school examinations. I went home a different person and began studying. I ended up passing my year 12 examinations and getting into university to study engineering.

I was so proud of myself because I thought I had made it through the hardest thing I would ever have to face in my life. However, I was wrong.

During my first year as an engineering student, I started exercising at the university gymnasium. This helped me build muscle and confidence. This confidence enabled me to go out socializing with friends at night clubs, sometimes up to 6 times a week.

While I was out socializing, I would often be thinking that I should be studying and when I was studying I would often be thinking about going out socializing. Somehow my wires got crossed. I was not focused on what I was doing in the moment. This lack of focus and all the going out resulted in my marks dropping. Luckily, I managed to scrape through to the second year.

In my second year, the course got even harder. It was at this point that I realized I had not made it and that this engineering course was more difficult than I had expected. Then, during my first semester exams, my father got sick and had to go to the hospital for an operation. He had the operation and returned back to a normal hospital ward. I thought he was going to be fine.

Then we got a call from the hospital saying he had to be moved back into the intensive care unit as something was wrong. Unfortunately, he ended up dying and I ended up failing some of my exams. This was the lowest point in my life. I felt depressed and alone. I felt that I had let myself and my father down. I thought my father died not being proud of me.

I spent the next day in the park alone, crying my eyes out. I did not know what to do.

I knew that I would probably have to repeat the year. I also knew that the odds were against me as, statistically, 240 students entered the first year and only 120 graduated after their fourth year. That is a fifty percent dropout rate. I thought, *should I just take the easy option and give up?* Then I thought of what my father would say.

I imagined him saying, in a loud and angry voice, "Get up you bum and stop crying because your Dad loves you! Finish your studies and become the best person you can be. Live a good life."

After all, that is why he made a sacrifice and took the risk in the first place to come to Australia. He wanted to give us all a better life.

At that moment, I felt this power inside of me I cannot explain. I wanted to make sure he did not die for no reason. I felt I had, at that moment, what is described in the movie *Rocky 3* as "the eye of the tiger" and nothing was going to stop me from graduating. I went forward believing I could do it and I did it. I got my Bachelor degree in engineering and a job to follow.

A few years later, I met a beautiful woman; we got married and had three wonderful children.

I worked for 18 years in a large company until they decided to restructure and, as a result, I lost my job. I then found another job and worked there for 7 years. Overall, I enjoyed most of my 25 years working as an engineer and people manager. However, in the last few years I noticed that my enjoyment had started to decline.

I noticed that I had become a person who valued image, position, power, control, ego and money, and, as a result, I felt unhappy, unfulfilled, uninspired, and my life lacked meaning and direction. I could not go on like this, something had to change.

I practiced some introspection and realized that I had a passion for personal development and helping others live a happier life. So, I decided to go back to school and become a professional life coach.

Today my values are health, family, friends, contribution, freedom and fun, and, as a result, I feel happy, fulfilled, inspired, inner peace, and that my life has meaning and direction. I love my life!

My passion is to inspire people to do what they love that also contributes to humanity; to help people create a life they love; to help people find their passion, develop it and give it to the world.

I imagine a world in which everyone loves Mondays because they love what they do and, more importantly, they are proud of whom they have become.

I invite you to be part of a community of people who live passionately, express themselves and strive to make this a better world.

I am truly thankful for the life I live. I love learning and sharing what I learn so others can benefit. I believe the meaning of life is to grow as an individual so you can help others. To be like a fruit tree that grows and bears fruit for others. That is the secret to a happy life.

Thank you for taking the time to read my story.

Wishing you a life you love!
Martin Formato

PS. If at any point while you are reading this guide you have any questions, please do not hesitate to contact me at **martin@martinformato.com** .

THANKFUL LIST

Research tells us that people crave the following:
A holiday
Chocolate and ice-cream
To be appreciated
True friendship
Laughter
To be touched
To find a partner they love
Losing oneself in the music
A fulfilling job
Success
Thighs that do not touch
Companionship
To be happy and healthy
To be true to themselves
To challenge themselves
To be creative
Self-worth
Sleep
Good food

Simplicity
Freedom
Wisdom
Massages
Art
A hug
Being outside in nature
To feel significant
To see how far they can go
To be inspired
A new level of confidence
To be heard
Nice clothes
Peace
Free time
A career that they love
To be loving and generous
To have some fun
Recognition
Rewarding work
To make a difference in someone's life
To know their life has meaning and purpose
To be deeply satisfied that the day was lived well
To find a way to express themselves
To make a living doing what they love
To accomplish their dreams

After all basic needs are met (health, food, water, shelter etc.), the reason why people are not happy is because they are not living a purposeful or passionate life. That is, their life has no meaning, no direction. They become lethargic, lazy, bored and depressed.

Research shows that those who have a life purpose or passion know where they are going, have less stress, more energy and live longer.

Imagine a world where everyone loved Mondays because they were living their life's purpose, their passion, their gift.

People who love their life are expressing themselves through their passion.

The only way to create a life you love is by finding your passion, developing it through self-improvement and giving it to the world.

YOU ARE A GIFT

You are a gift to the world.

You are unique. There will never be another you.

The world needs that gift that only you can give.

If you had the cure for cancer would you keep it all to yourself or would you give it to the world? Of course you would give it to the world.

The same goes with your gift or passion. Do the right thing and give it to the world.

Your creator does not make mistakes. You have a gift or passion. It is your duty to find it and give it to the world. This is the only way you will experience true happiness.

Material things do not bring you lasting happiness.

Becoming who you are capable of will bring you lasting happiness.

It is the journey, the progress, the growth which will bring you the most joy.

Your life is 99% the journey, so enjoy it doing what you love, your passion.

The way to do this is through finding, developing and living your passion. Do not settle for less than you can be.

You alone need to decide what your passion or purpose is. I cannot tell you what it is. Only you know what it is. You are the expert in your life.

By you deciding, you create it and you own it. It is yours.

This is a very important step that only you can take. You need to freely decide.

Your passion or purpose in life is closely interwoven with your value system. Values are something we instinctly move towards prompted from within.

Finding your passion or purpose is very important as it satisfies a core human need and that is to have certainty or stability and gives your life direction especially in this constantly changing world.

Once your passion or purpose is known then you can spend your time and energy developing it as opposed to still searching for it.

Your passion is your inner fuel which drives you; it is also your rock, your foundation, your home.

It gives your life meaning. More importantly it gives you a meaning, it gives you an identity.

Living your passion enables you to enjoy the journey. It is not something that you enjoy only at the end when you achieve it.

There needs to be a meaning to who you believe you are here to become.

A life without meaning is painful. It is like being lost and afraid.

I believe everything happens for a reason. We are here for a reason. It is your duty to find out and to find out quickly so you can become that person (develop yourself) and behave like that person (through your special contributions).

3 STEPS TO CREATE A LIFE YOU LOVE

Step 1: Find your **PASSION**

Step 2: **DEVELOP** your passion (Self-Improvement)

Step 3: **GIVE** your passion to the world

This is the meaning of life; to use your passion to GROW and CONTRIBUTE, to make yourself and others happy.

To grow is to learn, develop and improve yourself. To raise your standards.

To contribute is to give to and help others.

Be like a fruit tree, grow and bear fruit for others.

Congratulations, you have found the answer to the meaning of life.

Now, forget what you are supposed to do or what others expect you to do.

Stop everything and listen to your inner voice. Stop living unconsciously as if you have all the time in the world.

Start reflecting on your life and decide who you want to be, what you want to do and where you want to go. Have this end in mind.

You do not want to wake up after 50 years to find that you have lived someone else's life and not your own.

Do what you want to do. Live your own life the way you want to live it.

The realm of possibilities exists inside your mind. You are free to choose.

If you want to be a teacher, then go learn how to teach.

If you want to play the guitar, then go learn how to play the guitar.

If you want to cook, then go learn how to cook.

If you want to be an engineer, then go learn engineering.

It is that simple.

Just **decide**!

Life is too short. You do not have time to waste.

In the end, as you take your last breath, you do not want to have regrets.

You do not want to discover that you actually lived someone else's life.

You need to be satisfied knowing that you truly lived your life your way.

Once you have decided what your life's purpose or passion is, then you need to improve yourself so you can move towards living it.

The only way you can improve yourself is by becoming a student. That is what self-improvement is all about, being a student.

Now, to be the best you can be, you need to become the best student you can be.

Remember, Leaders and Winners are learners. Losers think they know it all.

To guarantee your happiness today, tomorrow and in the end, you need to have your very own motivating life purpose or passion and, through self-improvement, you need to take the necessary action to move towards living it.

Step 1: Find your PASSION

Take some time to write down the answers to these important questions.

It will really help you realize your life's purpose or passion.

What am I passionate about?

What do I love doing in my spare time (hobbies)?

What did I want to do and be as a child?

What subjects or activities did I enjoy most in school?

If I had only 3 months left to live, what would I do?

For example: Quit my job, devote more time to family and friends, spend 2 weeks in Paris, write up my will, live it up.

What would I like to leave the world as my legacy?

If I won the lottery, what would I do?

If I had no fear, what would I do?

How would I describe the perfect day for me?

What challenges have I overcome and would like to help others overcome too?

What am I really proud of?

What am I usually doing when I suddenly realise that time has flown by, and all my focus has been on that one task?

Who do I admire and why?

What do I most regret not doing, so far in my life?

What makes me happy?

What do people ask me for help with?

What am I good at, that others may have told me?

What would I do if you knew I could not fail?

If I had a magic wand what would I change about the world?

What types of books do I like to read?

What work would I do for free?

How would I like to be remembered?

What do I search for on the internet?

What type of work would give my life meaning?

Now that you have answered all these questions please review your answers.

What would you say is your life's purpose or passion?

Take your best guess for now, just to get started with something that excites you. Soon you will know if it is the right one.

For example: My passion is to inspire as many people as possible to do what they love that also contributes to humanity; to inspire people to express themselves through their passion by first helping them find their purpose or passion, then develop it and then give it to the world. I do this through coaching.

I help people find their gift, passion and purpose so they can start doing work that matters and as a result feel fulfilled, healthy and live longer.

Now it's your turn...

My Passion or life's purpose is:

I help people   so they can

What do I get from living my passion?

Will my passion make other people so happy that they would pay me to give it to them? If yes, then you could make a living out of your passion.

How do I feel about my passion?

Does my passion inspire me?

Well done on completing Step 1 and congratulations on finding your life's PURPOSE, your PASSION, your GIFT!

Step 2: DEVELOP your passion (Self-Improvement)

By becoming a student of your purpose, passion, gift (your craft), you will gain the necessary knowledge, skills and experience to become an expert or master of your craft which will enable you to produce a product or provide a service that will be highly valued by other people, something that people will pay you dearly for.

So go ahead and take massive action as, without action, nothing happens.

Only you can take the necessary action. No-one else can do it for you.

It is like exercising to become fit. Only you can do the exercise, no one else can do it for you.

In addition it is fun acquiring new knowledge and skills and it will do wonders for your confidence.

Your family and friends will notice the difference. They will see that you are someone going somewhere.

Can you do it?

Yes you can!

You can surprise everyone.

Or you can just sit back and let your potential waste away.

The choice is yours.

Step 3: GIVE your passion to the world

As you are developing your passion (your gift), you can give it for free to others or you can charge them for the privilege or do a bit of both. The choice is yours.

In my new book, "**How To Find Happiness**", I go into greater detail on:

How to create a life you love
How to understand yourself better
How you think, feel and why you do things
How to stay motivated and inspired to improve every aspect of your life
How to take control of your life so you can enjoy the journey
How to overcome limiting beliefs and daily challenges

"**How To Find Happiness**" contains a section of over 50 pages just on techniques and strategies for coaching yourself to success.

Let us face it, if you do not take action now where will you be in 12 months' time? Will you be richer, wiser, happier, and more successful ... or will you just be another year older?

LIFE IS SHORT

Remember you are dying.

There are a limited number of tomorrows.

Do now, do not wait.

It is not important how long you are going to live; it is important how you are going to live.

Just like it is not important how long you are at work, but what you do at work.

For fulfilment there needs to be meaning in what you do.

Give this moment meaning.

Give the next hour meaning.

Give your day meaning.

Give this year meaning.

Give your life meaning.

You are unique, you are special. There will never be another you. What you can contribute no-one else can.

You are a gift to the world.

You have something special to give, something that you are passionate about.

Do not keep it all to yourself, share it. The world needs you.

Most people want to experience love, happiness and success.

The only way is by your living your passion through hard work, dedication and a good attitude.

Lose yourself in what you love, your passion.

You are capable. Never give up; never lose hope, rest if you must.

Fear can hold you prisoner. Courage can set you free.

The Pygmalion effect occurs when our expectations unconsciously influence the outcome.

That is, when you expect and see yourself doing well, you do well.

So expect the best and the best will manifest itself.

Expect yourself living your passion and you will live your passion.

CONCLUSION

Thank you again for purchasing this book!

I hope this book was able to help you change your life.

I appreciate you for taking the time out of your day or evening to read this book, and if you have an extra second, I would love to hear what you think about this book or answer any questions.

Please shoot me an email at **martin@martinformato.com** . I read each and every single email!

I hope you have enjoyed this book as much as I loved writing it for you.

If you enjoyed this book, then I would like to ask you a favor. Would you be kind enough to leave a review for this book on Amazon? I would greatly appreciate it!

Go here: http://amzn.to/1rvHrhq

Also if you liked and got value from my book and want more tips on how to Create a Life You Love then please like and subscribe to my other channels below.

Facebook: http://www.facebook.com/doingworkthatmatters

Twitter: http://twitter.com/WorkThatMatter

Instagram: http://www.instagram.com/doing_work_that_matters

Amazon Kindle Books: http://www.amazon.com/Martin-Formato/e/B00M45LI3W

YouTube: https://www.youtube.com/channel/UC_ehfAiip7cBUo-bSdm2uDw

Hopefully by now you feel excited and passionate about your future.

If you liked my writing style, you would absolutely love my new book, "**Follow Your Own Path**".

This is the coolest book I have ever been involved in and by purchasing a copy you put another copy into the hands of someone less fortunate and you also help me with my mission which is to inspire people to do what they love that also contributes to humanity. That is a win/win/win.

Who Is This Book For?

This book is for anyone who is hungry.
Anyone who wants more out of life.
Anyone who knows that they have more to give, share and experience.
Anyone who feels deep down, in their heart, that they are here for a reason.
It's a book for people who feel stuck, lost, depressed or even suicidal.
In particular, it's for, entrepreneurs who are struggling, school leavers who are lost, employees who are bored or in a job they hate and redundees who feel discarded.
Today, more than ever in history, people need more direction and less information.
This book will put you on the right path, YOUR PATH.

Who Is This Book NOT For?

You should not get this book until you are certain that you truly wish to change your life and you are 100 percent committed to it.

Ask yourself these 2 questions:

Do I want to make a change voluntarily, completely of my own choice?
Do I really want to change my life?

If you cannot honestly say "Yes" without hesitation to both questions, then it is better that you wait until you are serious about changing your life.
As one monk famously said "We want only warriors… victims need not apply".

Go here to get your copy of "Follow Your Own Path"

http://amzn.to/2kQC9CK

If the links do not work, for whatever reason, you can simply search for the title "Follow Your Own Path" on the Amazon website.

Thank you again, and I wish you nothing less than a life you love!

Martin Formato

Email: martin@martinformato.com
Website: www.martinformato.com

Contents from my book "Follow Your Own Path"

STEP 3: GIVE YOUR PASSION TO THE WORLD

To get my book go to http://amzn.to/2kQC9CK

If the links do not work, for whatever reason, you can simply search for the title "Follow Your Own Path" on the Amazon website.

15 BONUS FREE BOOK

Go to my website at www.martinformato.com and enter your email address to get my FREE book **"Find Your Gift, Passion and Purpose"**.

Once you register you will be sent FREE information that will further help you create a life you love.

All you have to do is enter your email address to get instant access.

This information will help you get more out of your life – to be able to reach your goals, have more motivation, be at your best, and live the life you have always dreamed of.

I am continually adding new resources, which you will be notified of as a subscriber. These will help you live your life to the fullest!

To get instant access to these incredible tools and resources go to www.martinformato.com

16 ABOUT THE AUTHOR

Hi, I'm Martin Formato, a professional certified life and business coach, motivational speaker and author of the self-help book, "Follow Your Own Path".

My passion is to inspire you to do what you love that also contributes to humanity. How? By helping you express yourself through your passion.

This process will inevitably result in you creating a life you love.

How would you like to jump out of bed every Monday morning, full of excitement about the day ahead because you a living your life with passion and purpose?

I believe that you are a gift to the world and have a passion, gift, talent, skill or ability of some sort, which, once discovered and developed, will open up a whole new, amazing and wonderful world.

What you can contribute no-one else can contribute, because you are unique.

I want to help you find your passion and develop it so you can give it to the world. Why? Because:

I get a buzz helping people transform their life,

The world needs that special something that only you can give,

You deserve to be happy and when you express yourself through your passion you will be happy,

You will love what you do every day and who you are becoming and in the process

You will create a life you love.

By living your passion, you will also be setting an example for your family and friends to do the same. You will inspire them to also go after their dream.

I imagine a world where most people love Mondays because they love what they do; they express themselves through their passion, they help others and fulfill their dream. It doesn't get any better than that!

My blog at www.martinformato.com is my way of sharing ideas, concepts and principles that I have learnt over the last 50 years, which, if acted upon, will allow you to create a life you love. I am sharing this information as my way of giving back to society.

I am thankful to all those men, women and children that I have met throughout my life; some still living and others deceased; the authors of numerous books I have read; seminars I attended; movies and videos I have watched; audios I have listened to; and especially my parents, sister and brothers, my wife, children and relatives for teaching and helping me to shape the person I have become.

It does not matter if you are struggling or doing well, I guarantee that you will learn something from my blog that will make your life better.

My passion is to inspire people to do what they love that also contributes to humanity; to help people create a life they love; to help people find their passion, develop it and give it to the world.

I imagine a world in which everyone loves Mondays because they love what they do and, more importantly, they are proud of whom they have become.

I invite you to be part of our community of people who live passionately, express ourselves and strive to make this a better world.

I am truly thankful for the life I live. I love learning and sharing what I learn so others can benefit. I believe the meaning of life is to grow as an individual so you can help others. To be like a fruit tree that grows and bears fruit for others. That is the secret to a happy life.

Thank you for taking the time to read my message.

Wishing you a life you love!

Martin Formato

PS. If at any point you have any questions, please do not hesitate to contact me. You can best reach me on my blog at www.martinformato.com or simply email me at martin@martinformato.com . Even if you do not have any questions, I would love for you to come by and say hello!